The Life of

Asa Candler

and the story of Coca-Cola®

Rebecca Vickers

www.heinemann.co.uk/library

Visit our website to find out more information about **Heinemann Library** books.

To order:
 Phone 44 (0) 1865 888066
Send a fax to 44 (0) 1865 314091
 Visit the Heinemann Bookshop at www.heinemann.co.uk/library to browse our catalogue and order online.

First published in Great Britain by Heinemann Library, Halley Court, Jordan Hill, Oxford OX2 8EJ, part of Harcourt Education.
Heinemann is a registered trademark of Harcourt Education Ltd.

Editorial: Traci Todd and Harriet Milles
Design: Richard Parker and Maverick Design
Picture Research: Jill Birschbach
Production: Camilla Smith

Originated by Repro Multi-Warna
Printed and bound in China by
    South China Printing Company

The paper used to print this book comes from sustainable resources.

ISBN 0 431 18098 9
09 08 07 06 05
10 9 8 7 6 5 4 3 2 1

British Library Cataloguing in Publication Data
Rebecca Vickers
Asa Candler. – (The Life of)
338. 7'6632'092
A full catalogue record for this book is available from the British Library.

Acknowledgements
The Publishers would like to thank the following for permission to reproduce photographs:
p. 4 Kalish/DiMaggio/Corbis; pp. **5, 16** John Van Hasselt/Corbis Sygma; pp. **6, 12, 13, 25** Special Collections Department, Robert W. Woodruff Library, Emory University; pp. **7, 18, 21, 22** Bettmann/Corbis; pp. **8, 24** Corbis; pp. **9, 10, 11, 14, 15, 19** Courtesy, Georgia Archives; pp. **17, 20** The Advertising Archive Ltd.; p. **23** Underwood & Underwood/Corbis; p. **26** Ken Straton/Corbis; p. **27** ChromoSohm Inc./Corbis

Cover photograph by John Van Hasselt/Corbis Sygma
Cover and interior icons Janet Lankford Moran/Heinemann Library

Coca-Cola® is the registered trademark of The Coca-Cola Company

Every effort has been made to contact copyright holders of any material reproduced in this book. Any omissions will be rectified in subsequent printings if notice is given to the Publishers.

Disclaimer
All the Internet addresses (URLs) given in this book were valid at the time of going to press. However, due to the dynamic nature of the Internet, some addresses may have changed, or sites may have changed or ceased to exist since publication. While the author and Publishers regret any inconvenience this may cause readers, no responsibility for any such changes can be accepted by either the author or the Publishers.

Contents

Words shown in the text in bold, **like this**, are explained in the Glossary

A drink for the world

Soft drinks are sold in cans and bottles all over the world. They come in hundreds of different flavours. The most famous soft drink is Coca-Cola.

Today The Coca-Cola **Company** makes many different drinks.

Coca-Cola was first made about 120 years ago. Then, it was sold as a drink to make people feel better. Asa Candler started the company that put Coca-Cola into bottles and sold it around the world.

Asa Candler's company made the most famous soft drink in the world.

Early years

Asa Candler was born on 30 December 1851, near Villa Rica, Georgia, USA. Asa's father was an important farmer. His mother looked after their eleven children.

Here is a picture of Asa when he was a young child.

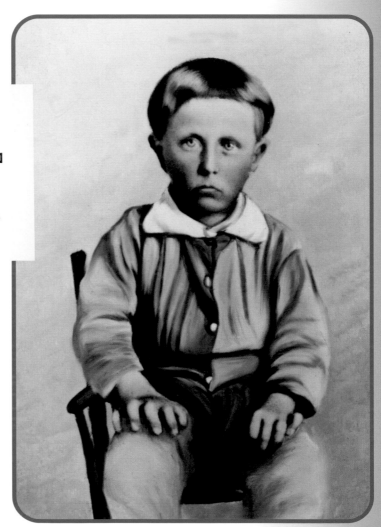

Asa sold his furs in shops like this one.

When Asa was a young boy, he sold animal furs and bought pins with the money he made. Asa then sold the pins to make more money.

A wartime childhood

Asa went to school in Villa Rica, Georgia. When he was nine years old, the **American Civil War** started. There were many fierce battles in Georgia.

Towns like Atlanta in Georgia were in ruins after the Civil War.

Asa missed a lot of school during the war. He only went to school for two years. Then he got a job as an **apprentice** in a chemist shop in Cartersville, Georgia.

This is Cartersville in Georgia. Asa worked here for a **pharmacist** in a chemist shop.

Moving to the city

After nearly three years in Cartersville, Asa got a new job in a shop in Atlanta. Atlanta is the **capital** city of Georgia.

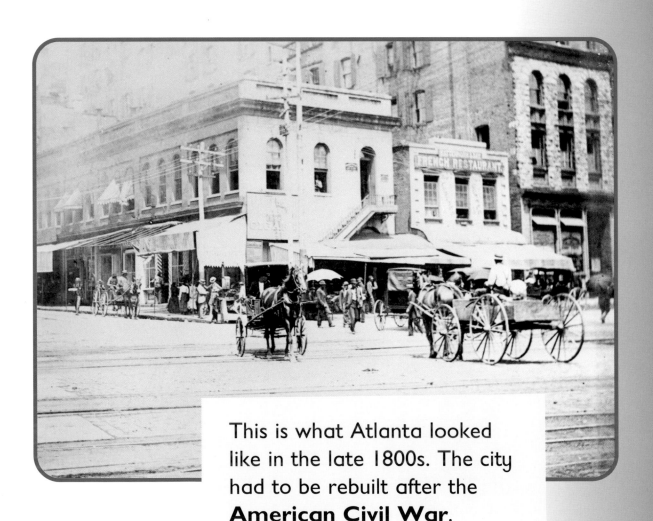

This is what Atlanta looked like in the late 1800s. The city had to be rebuilt after the **American Civil War**.

Young men worked in chemist shops, mixing medicines, serving drinks, and helping **customers**.

Dr George J. Howard owned chemist shops in Atlanta. Asa worked in one of them for a while.

A young businessman

Asa worked for Dr Howard for a few years. Then Asa and his friend, Marcellus Hallman, bought one of Dr Howard's shops.

This is a photo of one of Asa's shops in Atlanta.

When he was 26 years old, Asa married Dr Howard's daughter, Lucy. In 1881, he bought Marcellus's share of the **business**. Now Asa had his own shops!

Asa and Lucy lived in this house in Atlanta.

Family life

Asa and Lucy's first son, Charles Howard, was born in December 1878. Asa was very successful. He bought more **businesses** and made a lot of money.

Asa and Lucy had four sons and one daughter.

Asa went to a local church like this one.

Religion was very important to Asa. As well as being a **businessman**, he was also a Sunday school teacher.

Pemberton's formula

In 1886, an Atlanta **pharmacist** called John S. Pemberton **invented** a new **tonic** drink to make people feel better.

This is a photo of John S. Pemberton. He made **formulas** for many medicines and drinks.

Pemberton's **bookkeeper**, Frank Robinson, called this new drink Coca-Cola. He wrote down the name in curly handwriting. The new drink was very popular.

Frank Robinson chose the name Coca-Cola, and designed the way to write it.

A new company

Asa knew about Pemberton and his drinks. He thought that Coca-Cola could be a success. Asa bought Pemberton's **formula**.

This is Marietta Street in Atlanta. This is where Coca-Cola was first made and put into bottles.

In the early 1900s, Coca-Cola was delivered in carts like this one.

Asa wanted Coca-Cola to be sold to people everywhere. He started The Coca-Cola **Company**, to make and sell the drink.

Big business

Asa was right about Coca-Cola. A lot of people liked it and wanted to buy it. He had to open big **factories** to make as much as he could.

In 1916, the bottle shape on the right was chosen to be the only style of Coca-Cola bottle.

Asa made sure that people knew about his drink by using **advertising**.

Asa wanted people all over the USA to know about Coca-Cola. He used salespeople, and advertised in magazines and newspapers.

Success and problems

The Coca-Cola **Company** was very successful. By 1900, Asa was selling the drink all over the USA. But the company did have some problems.

This is an early **advertisement** for Coca-Cola.

After 1909, Coca-Cola was sold just as a soft drink – not a tonic.

In 1909, the US government said that Coca-Cola might not be good for people. Asa agreed to make changes. Coca-Cola was now advertised just as a soft drink, not a **tonic** or medicine.

Handing over control

By 1915, Coca-Cola was for sale in many places in the USA. In 1917, Asa gave the **company** to his children.

In the early 1900s, Asa and Lucy went to Europe for a long holiday. This is a picture of Paris, France, at that time.

This is Asa and Lucy's house in Atlanta, Georgia. Asa was **mayor** of Atlanta from 1916 to 1918.

Asa's wife Lucy died in March 1919. In September 1919, Asa's children sold the company. Asa was very unhappy about this. He died in 1929.

More about Asa

Asa Candler made Coca-Cola a popular drink all over the world. The **company** is now very big. Today, you can buy Coca-Cola in almost 200 countries.

Now people all over the world drink Coca-Cola. Here it is **advertised** in Tokyo, Japan.

People have written books about the story of Asa Candler and his company. There is a Coca-Cola **museum** in Atlanta, Georgia.

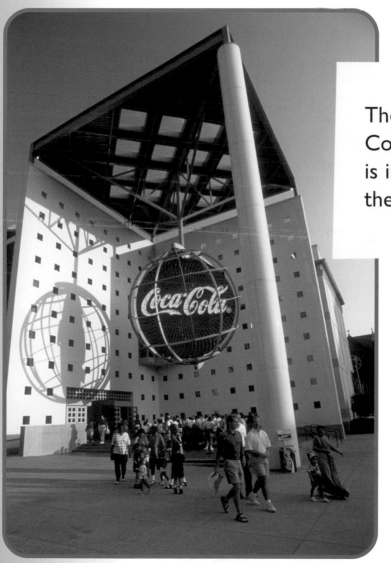

The World of Coca-Cola Museum is in Atlanta, where the company started.

Fact file

- Asa's father, Sam Candler, gave the town of Villa Rica its name. Villa Rica means 'rich village' in Spanish.

- Asa Candler was very small. He was just a little over 1.5 metres tall. He was known for his high, squeaky voice.

- Santa Claus is usually shown as a chubby, happy person in a red suit, trimmed with white fur. This is because the Coca-Cola **advertisements** in 1931 made him look like that.

- 'Coca-Cola' is the second most-recognized word in the world. The most-recognized word is 'okay'.

Timeline

1851	Asa Candler is born on 30 December
1870	Asa becomes an **apprentice** at a chemist shop in Cartersville, Georgia
1873	Asa moves to Atlanta, Georgia
1878	Asa marries Lucy Howard
1881	Asa starts his own **company**
1886	John S. Pemberton **invents** the Coca-Cola **formula**
1887	Asa buys the formula for Coca-Cola
1892	Asa starts The Coca-Cola Company
1899	Coca-Cola in bottles is sold in many places
1917	Asa Candler gives his children the company
1919	Lucy Candler dies. The family sells The Coca-Cola Company
1929	Asa Candler dies

Glossary

advertising/ advertisement show or tell people about something they can buy

apprentice someone who works for a person while learning their job

bookkeeper person who keeps the money records for a company

business activity that earns money

businessman person who works in a business

capital city where the government is based

American Civil War war from 1861 to 1865 between the northern states and the southern states of the USA

company group of people who make money by selling things

customers people who buy goods

factory place where things are made

formula method and ingredients to make something

inventing making something that has never been made before

mayor person who is head of a town or city

museum place where important parts of history are kept

pharmacist someone who mixes and sells medicines

tonic liquid that people drink, like a medicine

Find out more

Books
An older reader can help you with these books:

Coca-Cola, William Gould (Zero to Ten, 2005)

The Story of Coca-Cola, Lonnie Bell (Creative Publishing International, 2004)

Websites
www.coca-cola.co.uk
Find plenty of information on The Coca-Cola Company's own website.

Places to visit
World of Coca-Cola
55, Martin Luther King, Jr. Drive
Atlanta 30303-3505, Georgia, USA

> Always remember that drinking too many sweet, fizzy drinks is bad for your health.

Index

Titles in *The Life of* series include:

Hardback   0 431 18073 3

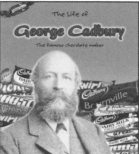

Hardback   0 431 18105 5

Hardback   0 431 18098 9

Hardback   0 431 18099 7

Hardback   0 431 18071 7

Hardback   0 431 18072 5

Hardback   0 431 18100 4

Hardback   0 431 18106 3

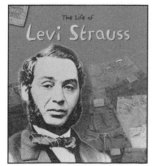

Hardback   0 431 18070 9

Hardback   0 431 18101 2

Find out about the other titles in the Heinemann Library on our website www.heinemann.co.uk/library